THE LAND OF TEARS

—IS A—

SECRET PLACE

Loss/Grief Support Journal Workbook

PATTY L. LUCKENBACH

ISBN: 978-1-956373-83-7 (sc)
ISBN: 978-1-956373-84-4 (hc)
ISBN: 978-1-956373-85-1 (e)

THE EWINGS PUBLISHING

The Ewings Publishing LLC
One Galleria Blvd., Suite 1900, Metairie, LA 70001
1-888-421-2397

This book belongs to

_____

DEDICATION

This book is dedicated to my brother, Bill, who was only seven years old when our father died; and in turn it is dedicated to each of you who is willing to step through your grieving heart. The doorway to the heart opens inward, so open your heart and sense the mansion of life within you. It has been my desire in writing this book that each of you will not avoid your grief, but commune with it, for it has so much to teach you about living.

ACKNOWLEDGMENTS

I extend special appreciation to my dear friends Kay Adams, Janet Patton, Marty Beadle, and Launa Fujimoto; colleague Jim McCartney; and my precious teacher, Claudia Helade, who believed in the work and in me. I gratefully appreciate the assistance given in synthesizing and editing this material.

The eagle looks for a storm and uses the pressure
of the raging storm to catch the edge of the storm to lift it higher.
This gives the eagle an opportunity to glide and rest. We can
use the storms of our lives to raise us to greater heights.

~ by Dr. Myler Monroe

CONTENTS

Chapter 1   Introduction..7

Chapter 2   Workbook 11

Chapter 3   Death 15

Chapter 4   Definitions...23

Chapter 5   Give Yourself to Journal.. 29

Chapter 6   Five Tasks of Mourning 39

Chapter 7   Grief Cycle 53

Chapter 8   Rituals..77

INTRODUCTION

Only people who avoid love

Can avoid grief

The point is to learn

From it and remain

vulnerable to love.

~John Brantner

Grief is a sense of separateness due to a death. Experiencing a death, whether physical death of a loved one or the death of a relationship, can be one of the most terrifying and, at the same time, most expanding events in your life.

There is a tightness of heart that we are left with after the experience of loss. The wound is the emotional pain of loss. The power to open ourselves to pain and mercy brings renewed understanding of life itself, and consequently compassion for ourselves and others.

It has long been my desire to assist individuals who have experienced the deep pain of adjustment necessitated by the separation through death from a loved one. Many times I have placed myself in the front lines of this work in order to grow and expand in the healing of my very own heart. I have felt pain, and I have known the inspiration that only comes from walking by someone's side as he/she loosens his/her heart and moves with the ebb and flow of life.

HOW TO USE *THE LAND OF TEARS IS A SECRET PLACE*

This Grief Support Journal Workbook is a gift. You might say it is a gift you give yourself. You can move through the book at your own pace, with space available for you to express yourself. The pages invite you to explore the process of mourning. So, please, each time you open the book, "listen." The pages will speak to you.

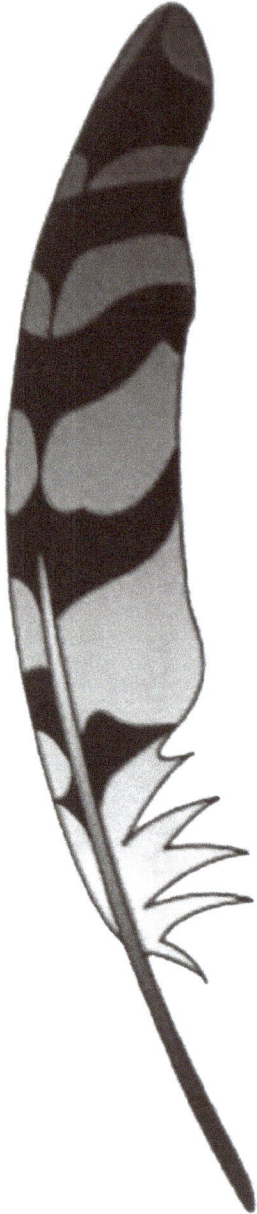

Let me be as feather
Strong, with purpose,
Yet light at heart
Able to bend.
And, tho I might
Become frayed,
Able to pull myself
Together again.

~Anita Sams

2 WORKBOOK

Life is short. It can come and go like a feather in the wind.

~Shania Twain

The workbook includes definitions of bereavement, grief, and mourning, healing, and an illustration of the grief cycle of transformation.

The definitions are here to explain how bereavement, grief, mourning and healing may be understood. The five tasks of mourning are defined and clarified.

The book also includes explanations of how writing in a journal can be a beautiful therapeutic tool for you in working through your grief. Permit me to say a few words about the tool of journaling (or writing down) your feelings and experiences. You have the freedom to write in your book however you choose. No one is grading it, analyzing it, correcting your spelling or checking for complete sentences. Here is your opportunity to express your feelings. There is no right or wrong to it. If you don't know how to get started, begin within the present moment or the present period. Begin, perhaps, by describing the present moment, a feeling, or a description.

Throughout this book are examples from my own journals and those of others as we work through our own bereavement and grief.

The journal process has been beneficial for me and for hundreds of others in aiding the understanding of and reorientation to life by taking the first step in acknowledging the loss and pain that come from losing something precious.

The material in this workbook has been prepared for you. It has been gathered together in the hope of assisting you in acknowledging your loss and in loosening the tightness of your heart.

Your journal workbook is your therapist; it awaits patiently for you to open and begin the journey. It will open up spaces between the words for you. You will have the opportunity in your book to clarify and define your very own meaning of loss and grief.

Yea, though I walk through the valley of the shadow of death, I will fear no evil; for thou art with me; thy rod and thy staff they comfort me.

3 DEATH

Death is a sense of being expanded.

~Claudia Helade

T believe you would agree with me that individuals who endure the experience of losing a loved one, whether husband, wife, parent, sibling, child or friend, need the ability to endure the presence of death in life. This is of decisive importance for human living. As Edgar Herzog says in *Psyche and Death*, "To open oneself to death is to accept the aspect of becoming, that is, of transformation, which is the very stuff of life, and so, at length, to realize that the human condition transcends itself." Is this the mystery of becoming?

There is a certain mystery about death that can't be explained, or perhaps never needs to be because it is a part of living. Science tells us that life, as energy, cannot be destroyed; however, energy does change form. No matter what religious canvas our life has been painted upon, as we search for the meaning of death, there is the sense that the woven canvas of life is a universal truth. We probably would all agree that what science realizes is true: death is merely the experience of changing form in an expansion of awareness.

Bare with me as I explore some analogies surrounding the death experience that relates to my experience of being present with individuals as they were dying. We speak about the ebb and the flow of life. In *Sympathetic Vibrations*, K.C. Cole says, "A vibration is a wiggle in time; a wave, a wiggle in space. A wave is not made of 'stuff'; it is a movement of information." A particle is manifested information (form), an abstract pattern. Cole invites us to consider that virtually everything around us, including ourselves, is essentially just such a pattern. It is the pattern of atoms and molecules that both defines a person and makes him or her precious.

Some people have used this analogy to explain how resonances can produce particles, according to Cole. First of all, a resonance determines what we see and what's reflected, and in the elementary universe of particle physics, every expression of energy is associated with a frequency, and vice versa. It is part of the natural complementarity of matter that it has both wave and particle characteristics.

Ernest Holmes, the founder of the Church of Religious Science, looked at the body as being composed of matter. Science tells us that matter is an aggregation of small particles arranged in some kind of form and it is in a continuous state of flow. Perhaps the wave Cole refers to is the buoyancy of life, which is invisible but every-sustaining. Our bodies are like a river, forever flowing and vibrating Life.

Do you suppose that the experience of death is like entering into a different vibration (experience), and when this occurs there is an awakening and a lightening of particles? Perhaps you set your personality (particle) aside and expand into the field of wave nature; this, I believe, is the expansion of consciousness. A perfect example of this is in birthing, whether it is birthing a living soul into this plane of existence or the birthing called death into the next plane of experience. Each experience is a rite of passage. Many people have called this experience "walking up beyond the dream."

So, if this is the case, why do we resist death? Is it because we don't sense the vibration of birthing and the continual expansion of life? Therefore, do we fear change? It seems that death is a healing into life. If this fundamental conclusion could be proven, would it not indicate that death is really all we know, for death is a change of form? We die daily to forms changing. So why do we resist death? Could it be because we hold onto form (particle) as our identity?

Death is spontaneous to all species of mammals on this planet. It is the human animal who emotionally attaches itself to things and other humans. I feel humans resist death because of the emotional buffering that surrounds physical attachments. In doing this the human loses sight of his primary instinctual responses of letting go.

We forget that to physically die is to be born by detaching and releasing the physical. The physical represents the particle and in birth we let go to the wave, "a wiggle in space." We lift the veil of unconsciousness to experience what is beyond the dream.

In childbirth the mother can be fearful because it is a seemingly unknown experience. But what does the baby experience? Does it ride the wave represented by the vibration of breath even as we are born into the experience of death and leave the form (particle)?

I have been with several people who have physically died. These experiences have reminded me of the labor of being born. Stephen Levine, in *Healing Into Life and Death,* puts it this way: "Healing into death, the separate self dissolves into universal being, seeing that any separation from life is a separation from healing."

There have been many experiences of individuals being unconscious (in a coma), and with only the sense of sound available to them. It seems that sound is the last known sense to go. It is the last to go because of the vibratory frequency, which rides the wave. Many times when the individuals become conscious they tell of having been with loved ones who have already died, and being aware of individuals on this plane at the same time. Are they in a state of being in two locations at once? They are experiencing the wave nature as they move awareness (consciousness) into a new pattern (field of energy) of awareness. I believe that consciousness is with us so that we may be the observer, for I see consciousness as the conduit of light.

Man needs to embrace the instinctual level, to uncover it from the subconscious levels, and then turn to it and learn the freedom of it. In doing this man can transmute the emotional barbs of his fear to ride the wave through the rite of passage of "waking up beyond the dream"—or death.

Now our intellect can accept that a form has changed, but we as individuals experience the adjustments of loosening the emotional pain of separateness. "Entering healing beyond ideas of life and death, we become who we have always been, that which preceded birth and survives death," according to Levine. Let us explore together this mystery called death and learn to ride the tide that brings each of us to the shores of peace and light.

The Waves sweeping in the sound of new birth. Holding to its grace. The waves wash the souls of our feet filling the souls of our hearts, touching the souls we shall meet, we shall meet—across the shore . We see the shadow of clouds hung high above our heads far below what God sees. This shore is ours to share. Now is our time. the Sun holding fast the gift of light giving to our eyes a vision of dream—singing. Through the silence for all who may listen, listen, listen to the Waves.

~From the song *The Wave*
Written by Rebecca Conly
& Kristopher Witty

Now it's time to begin exploring your own thoughts and feelings. Start right here, right now, and write a paragraph or two (or more if you wish) on this page and the next. Don't worry about doing it "right." Remember that you can't do it "wrong."

WHAT IS THE MEANING
OF DEATH TO ME?

"It is hard to have patience with people who say, 'There is no death,' or, 'Death doesn't matter.' There is death. And whatever is matters. And whatever happens has consequences, and it and they are irrevocable and irreversible."

~C.S.Lewis, *A Grief Observed*

4
DEFINITIONS

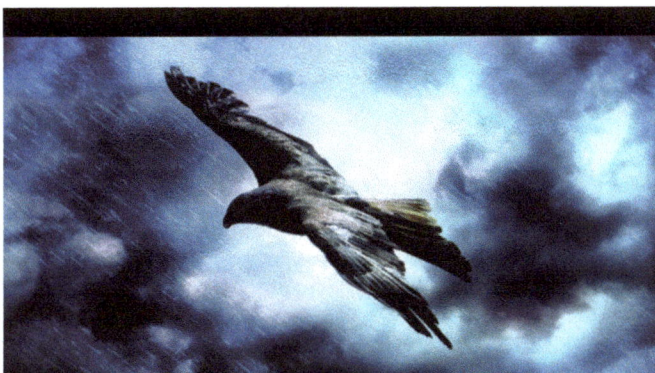

Feather to fire, fire to blood

Blood to bone, bone to morrow

Marrow to ashes, ashes to snow.

~Gregory Colbert

Healing is to make whole, to recognize the truth. What is the truth? It has been stated in the Bible that to know the truth sets one free. Could healing be the inward and outward sense of peace, assurance, gratitude, and love? Levine says in his book, *Healing Into Life And Death:*

> "Among the first steps of healing is to let go of our definition of what we imagined healing might be. Our healing is a meeting of the old with a newness. It is a letting go of the ancient numbness with which we react to our suffering, a relinquishment of clinging and identification with our incessant mercilessness and judgment, our momentous resistance and fear. It means not thinking our healing but being it." (p. 162)

Bereavement is a state caused by loss such as death. Numerous types of losses can bring about a state of bereavement. It is the experience of losing what we had and feeling grief for what we have lost.

Grief, as defined by Dr. Allan Wolfelt, director of The Center for Loss and Life Transitions of Fort Collins, Colorado, "is an emotional suffering caused by death or another form of bereavement. Grief involves a sequence of thoughts and feelings that follow loss and accompany mourning. Grief is a process and, as a result, is not a specific emotion like fear or sadness, but, indeed, is a constellation of a variety of thoughts, feelings, and behaviors. Grief is the internal meaning given to the external event."

Grief is a much more personal experience than words can describe. For example, grief is walking upstairs for the first time, grief is waking up in the middle of the night and reaching out to touch someone who is no longer there. Grief is hearing that special song, seeing that special place, and longing for that special person. And yes, grief is a mixture of adjustments, fears, and uncertainties that confront life in its forward progress and make it difficult to reconcile and redirect the energies of life: of living and loving.

Anticipatory Grief is most often used to describe grief that is expressed in advance of a loss when the loss is received as inevitable.

Acute Grief is the intense grief which immediately follows the loss.

My father died two days before my 11ᵗʰ birthday. I wish that someone then had given me a definition of grief. There were so many times when I absolutely didn't know what was the matter with me; furthermore, neither did my family or friends. Shouldn't I have gotten over my father's death by now? Why doesn't the world want to listen to me? I felt possessed by what had happened.

Grief is a universal experience. We see that grief is woven into the fabric of our identities. Grief takes our hand and leads us into the experience of opening our heart to the tender mercies of compassion. Take grief in and connect it to the bonding of wholeness. If we understand it, it will not devour us but set us free. The universal threads of true wholeness are golden, and they hold the quilt we call life together, no matter what color, texture, or age the fabric of your life is. Grief is an emotional journey that can result in a spiritual experience.

Mourning is a process that results from the universal experience of loss. It is a process that takes you on the journey from where you were before your loss to where you will be after you struggle and adapt to change in your life.

Mourning is the outward expression of grief and bereavement. The specific ways in which people mourn are influenced by the customs of their culture. The mourning behavior as exhibited may, or may not, be in agreement with the true feelings of the bereaved; however, they may incur disapproval if they do not follow the prescribed social customs. Another way of dealing with mourning is to state that it is "grief gone public," or "sharing one's grief outside of oneself."

Understanding mourning is no small task. It not only requires understanding how mourners grieve, how they react to change, and how physical and emotional functioning may become erratic, but it requires this understanding at a time when a person's usual perceptions, reasoning abilities, and ways of interpreting reality are distorted. Under the stress of loss, mourners may not see and hear accurately or be able to think clearly. Mourners are highly vulnerable, as much to events of their own making as to events forced upon them, as much to the consequences of their own feelings as to the desires of others.

The idea of mourning is extremely old and has been preserved in two of humanity's most ancient languages. Glen Davidson in his book, *Understanding Mourning,* says the root meaning in Sanskrit for mourning is "to remember" and in Greek it is "to care." The word is used to mean the way in which mourners adapt from what was to what is. To grieve (to be burdened by sorrow) and to be bereaved) to be robbed of someone or something precious) are only part of the mourning process.

"If there has been a bond there is grief."

~Claudia Helade

The sound of her skirt has stopped.

On marble pavement dust grows.

Her empty room is cold and still.

Fallen leaves are piled against the doors.

Longing for the lovely lady

How can I bring my aching heart to rest?

~Han Wu-Ti 157–87 B.C.

5
GIVE YOURSELF TO JOURNAL

The only thing I have done religiously in my life is keep a journal. I have hundreds of them, filled with feathers, flowers, photographs, and words—without locks, open on my shelves.

~Terry Tempest Williams

How Can Journaling Help Me?

The possible ways of looking at your life, and feeling its movement through writing, are infinite. Writing gives the unconscious mind the opportunity to speak. You can be aware of your participation in your grief process.

Journaling can assist in the reorientation of regret, anger, and release. It is a tool for facilitating communication and clarity, bringing forth forgiveness and peace of mind. It helps to deal with unfinished business and to work through it.

Journaling, as a therapeutic tool, provides a way to transmute energy in order to harvest the gifts of grief that move with the cycle of life.

Writing has not always been easy for me. In fact, I completely resisted it. As a child I experienced learning disabilities and to try to express myself through writing was scary for me. I lived with the fear that my work would be judged and was just not good enough. I was petrified to make an error, thinking, "Oh, what would they think?" It was through journaling that I was able to free myself from those old embedded patterns of thinking and discover and express my wellspring of creativity.

My journaling teacher, Kay Adams, once said to me, "You can't do it wrong. There are no mistakes. It's your book—yours alone. It can be neat or sloppy. You don't have to plan what you are going to do or say. You discover what you have done once you have set it down. Allow yourself to write whenever you feel like it: when you need the emotional release, when you need to clarify your thoughts." I gave myself permission to express myself, and it was true what Kay had said, there are no rules. You allow yourself to express yourself when you feel so inclined.

My journal has become one of my best friends. It certainly does not condemn me and it is always available. It is the canvas of my soul. Your journal can take on the role of minister, priest, counselor, friend, parent, child, or spiritual guide. Remember that the central relationship in the journal is with yourself.

It has been through journal writing that I have expressed my feelings and have dealt with my grief by telling my story. Everyone expresses his/her very own story and meaning. It is my deep desire that you will write down your feelings and tell your story. Telling the story helps, crying heals and lifts you to the point of discovery and gives permission for the continued exploration of life and death meanings.

Suggested Topics to Journal On

It is helpful to have what Kay Adams, in her book *Journal to the Self,* calls a Springboard. The Springboard is a word or phrase that helps you take the plunge into writing down your thoughts and feelings.

- WHAT HAS HAPPENED?
- MY TEARS ARE FROZEN. HOW DO I THAW THEM?
- IF I GAVE MYSELF PERMISSION TO CRY, I WOULD...
- I'LL WRITE A LETTER TO HIM/HER AND TELL HIM/ HER HOW I FEEL.
- I FEEL _____ ...
- I AM ANGRY BECAUSE:
- WHAT WOULD HE/SHE TELL ME TO DO NOW?
- I MISS ...
- WHAT I REMEMBER MOST ...

- WHO AM I, AND WHO WAS I BEFORE HE/SHE LEFT?
- HOW DO I SAY GOODBYE?
- WHERE AM I GOING?
- WHAT AM GOING TO DO?

Tools

Some helpful tools for you might be to start on the empty pages that follow and begin to list your feelings, NOW. Journalers refer to this technique as catharsis writing. "Cathartic writing is done under the pressure of intense emotion that calls for immediate expression. It could be as simple a statement as "I'm so angry!" says Rainer. It provides an emotional release. Put your scream into your book and slam it shut.

"The more deeply you can express your pain, the sooner you will work it through... Putting it into words begins the natural process of distancing yourself from it that finally brings relief."

*Your Pain is the breaking
of the shell that encloses
your understanding.*

~Kahlil Gibran, *The P rophet*

Give yourself permission to Grieve. You will not lose yourself but find yourself.

"Until we know our own brokenness
we know not compassion."

~Claudia Helade

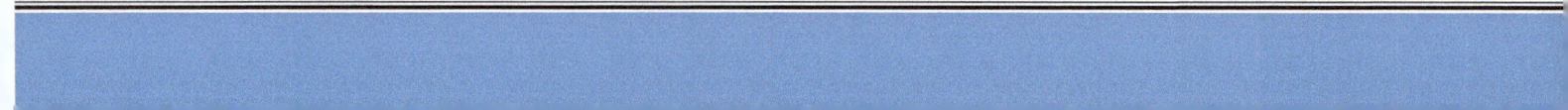

6
FIVE TASKS OF MOURNING

What good are wings without the courage to fly.

~Anthony

Five Tasks of Mourning

Wolfelt	Davidson
1. To express outside of oneself the reality of the death.	1. Accept the reality of the loss.
2. To tolerate the emotional suffering that is inherent in the work of grief while nurturing oneself both physically and emotionally.	2. Accept the pain of the loss.
3. To convert the relationship with deceased from one of the presence to a relationship of memory.	3. To adjust to an environment in which the deceased is missing.
4. To develop a new self-identity based on a life without the deceased.	4. To withdraw emotional energy and reinvest in other experiences and relationships.
5. To relate the experience of loss to a context of meaning.	5. To formulate and reap a spiritual harvest of understanding of immortality.

Glen W. Davidson, *Understanding Mourning* (Minneapolis, MN: Augsberg Pubishing House, 1984), pp. 30 – 33.

Alan D. Wolfelt, Ph.D., *Death and Grief: A Guide for Clergy* (Muncie, IN: Accelerated Development Inc., 1988), pp. 74 – 79.

Accept the Reality of the Loss

"The first task of mourning requires facing the reality that the loved one is dead," according to Davidson in *Understanding Mourning*. Many times our imagination leads us to unrealistic expectations. Only as imagination is confronted by realities are fantasies brought into control. Expressing the reality of the death by placing the experience in your journal can assist in cracking the seal of isolation.

The following was journaled by your author:

> He died two days before my birthday. I had attended my Girl Scout meeting where they had signed and given me a get-well card for my mother to take to the hospital for Dad. We had also celebrated my birthday at the meeting by having cupcakes for refreshments. I was instructed to walk to my grandparents' house after the Girl Scout meeting to wait for my mother to come from visiting Dad. My little brother was also told to go the Grandma's house right from school.
>
> As I entered my grandparents' house the feeling was heavier than lead. Grandma and Gramps just sat there with my brother. I remember I wanted to ask what was wrong, but I was afraid. It seemed like the four of us sat there forever. The thoughts that ran through my mind were, "I bet they told Mom that Dad would never walk again! Why isn't someone speaking?" As time went on, I only hoped that what they were preparing to tell us was, he would never walk again. That would be better than the dreadful thought that were beginning to paralyze my thinking and feeling.
>
> I believe it was my grandmother, holding my brother on her lap, who told us that shortly before we had arrived Mom had called from the hospital to say our father had died. My grandparents cried and I now recall that my brother and I just sat there in disbelief. I can't recall what was happening in my head. I do know I didn't cry or scream. I did not even question what

had been told to us. Looking back, it doesn't seem fair, I just accepted what they told us.

I recall that night at our house when relatives and friends came, how I could not cry; consequently, I felt like a freak. People didn't know what to say to my brother and me. They were trying to make everything OK. I wondered, "Is this really happening, or am I dreaming a nightmare?"

I waited years before I sat and entered this information on paper. Oh, how healing it would have been if I could have expressed myself then. It would have helped me work through my grief.

Some suggestions for entering into your journal are:

- Write a letter to someone who does not know about the death and give the details as to what has happened.

- Description writing is mainly reproducing reality as it is; you can include accounts of events, feelings, etc. In doing this you can preserve certain "unforgettable" perceptions against the annihilation of time.

The Garden

I came to an upturned soil left out in the air to die. It has been slow and painful and my remains have been vandalized. I have been dead for a long time and no one knew it. Is this garden finished? Where are the master gardeners? Who will feed it, water it, love it. Will the flower ever blossom? Will the garden put forth anything that will feed the soul of anyone!

~ From the journal of B.R.

Accept the Pain of Loss

The first step in healing is to acknowledge the pain; don't bury it in concrete. The second ask of mourning it to express the pain, anger, fear, or confusion. Working through the pain brings us into a shifting of our energies to re-connect with life.

My journal continued:

> Right before I was to go to bed, my mother broke away from the family members, entered my bedroom, and proceeded to give me the birthday present that both Mom and Dad had bought for me. It was a quilted skirt and blouse, white with the pattern of little black bows on it. She said he had picked it out. He would have wanted me to open it on my birthday. My emotions were numbed. What do you say? "Thanks a lot, but you shouldn't have done it." It was very emotional for my mother. I do know that once my bedroom light was turned off, I held my Raggedy Anne doll and cried for the first time, also the last for a long time.

> During the three days preceding the funeral, many gestures of love and concern were sent, such as food and flowers. I even received a little purple cow-planter with some flowers in it from my friends in the same Girl Scout troop that had previously sent home with me the get-well card for Dad. I guess the thing that really got to me was the birthday cake the girls in the neighborhood baked for me. Once again, the emotions continued to turn within me while I tried to make out that everything was OK. I received about five different cakes. I hate it when I saw someone else coming up the path with a cake. I felt like they were pitying me. Now I know it was their special way of participating in the grieving process.

> It appeared that my seven-year-old brother responded to our father's death by being sick to his stomach. When he wasn't vomiting, he was trying to be the center of attention I knew it was his way of calling out for help.

Looking back on things, I wish my brother and I could have held each other tight.

My aunt sat with me at the funeral. She held my hand as we gathered in front of the casket. There was a lot of commotion. I remember they gave my grandmother smelling salts. Everything seemed gray: Dad, the casket, the day. As I turned to walk from the casket I saw many people crying, but I still didn't cry. The cemetery was cold and snowy. By this time I had pretty much isolated my emotions.

A month and a half after Dad died, I became ill with a pain in my right side. I spent approximately two weeks in the hospital with a locked colon. It was not until I had been there a while that they discovered I had experienced a loss in my life. I remember the doctor emphasizing the importance for me to allow myself to cry and find an emotional release for the emotion.

If only years ago I could have expressed my feelings. Instead, I allowed those painful feelings to go underground within me, creating a fear of losing which began to demonstrate in later years through my relationships with men.

DON'T DISREGARD THE WOUND FOR IT WILL HEAL YOU

What I feel is:

"*No one ever told me that grief felt so like fear. I am not afraid, but the sensation is like being afraid. The same fluttering in the stomach, the same restlessness, the yawning. I keep on swallowing.*"

~ C.S. Lewis, *A Grief Observed*

Grief is the cry of emptiness of one's Soul, for which has been lost and will be no more. Grief is sadness and pain, despair and loneliness. A constellation of feelings and unbearable agony. Grief is like falling backwards into a dark hole.

Grief is sorrow! It is like waking up in the middle of the night and they are no longer next to you. Grief is learning to find yourself once again.

~ Beyond Loss Grief Support Group, 1990
Mile Hi Church

"Anger is wanting or not wanting something."

~ Dr. Thomas Hora

"We are healed of a suffering only by experiencing it to the fullest."

~ Marcel Proust

7

GRIEF CYCLE

Flight without feather is not easy.

~Plautus

The Cycle of Transformation

"That your passion may live through its own daily resurrection, and like the phoenix rise above its own ashes."

~ The Prophet

The cycle of grief is a cycle of transformation. This cycle reveals the possibility of movement and change. An excellent example of the cycle of transformation is found in nature with its four seasons. Each season holds within itself certain characteristics: dormancy, regeneration, warmth of growth, and harvest. What the cycle represents is the consistency of change. I recognize that the cycles of life include death. Life is not separate from death. The cycle of transformation is a continual cycle of death and rebirth on all levels.

My understanding of the transformational cycle has expanded my capacity to understand death and birth. We can look at the cycle of grief (transformation) and see how our perceptions change. One thing that nature teaches us is the consistency of change, and in acknowledging the process we become aware of our willingness to allow it to unfold in our lives.

When we think about it, every time we make a choice there is a death, because there is a change of thought that results in a change of form. We die to our limitations and our perceptions. We lose much of what we have been so that we may move into the realm of possibilities. Grief is like a rosebud, now tight, but in the process of unfolding.

One thing that we know for sure is the reliability of change in our lives, and when we cling to what changes we suffer. Steven Levine in his book, *Who Dies,* says:

> "We don't trust the sense of endlessness, of edgelessness within. Our suffering is caused by holding to how things might have been, should have been, could have been. Grief is part of our daily existence. But we seldom recognize that pain in our heart that one fellow called a deep weeping, a mourning for everything we have left behind."

LOSS

THE GRIEF CYCLE OF TRANSFORMATION

"Until we know our own brokenness, we know not compassion"

RECOVERY

New Spirituality

Commitment to Life

Focus on Present Service

Compassion

Increased Sensitivity

New Awareness

wOpen Heart

PROTEST

Denial

Unfairness

Anger

Shock

Numbness

Fear

DETACHMENT

Decreased Socialization

Short Attention Span

Lack of Patience

Depression

DESPAIR

Wanting to Die

Feelings of Insanity

Anger

Guilt

Helpnessness

Nothing will be the

same

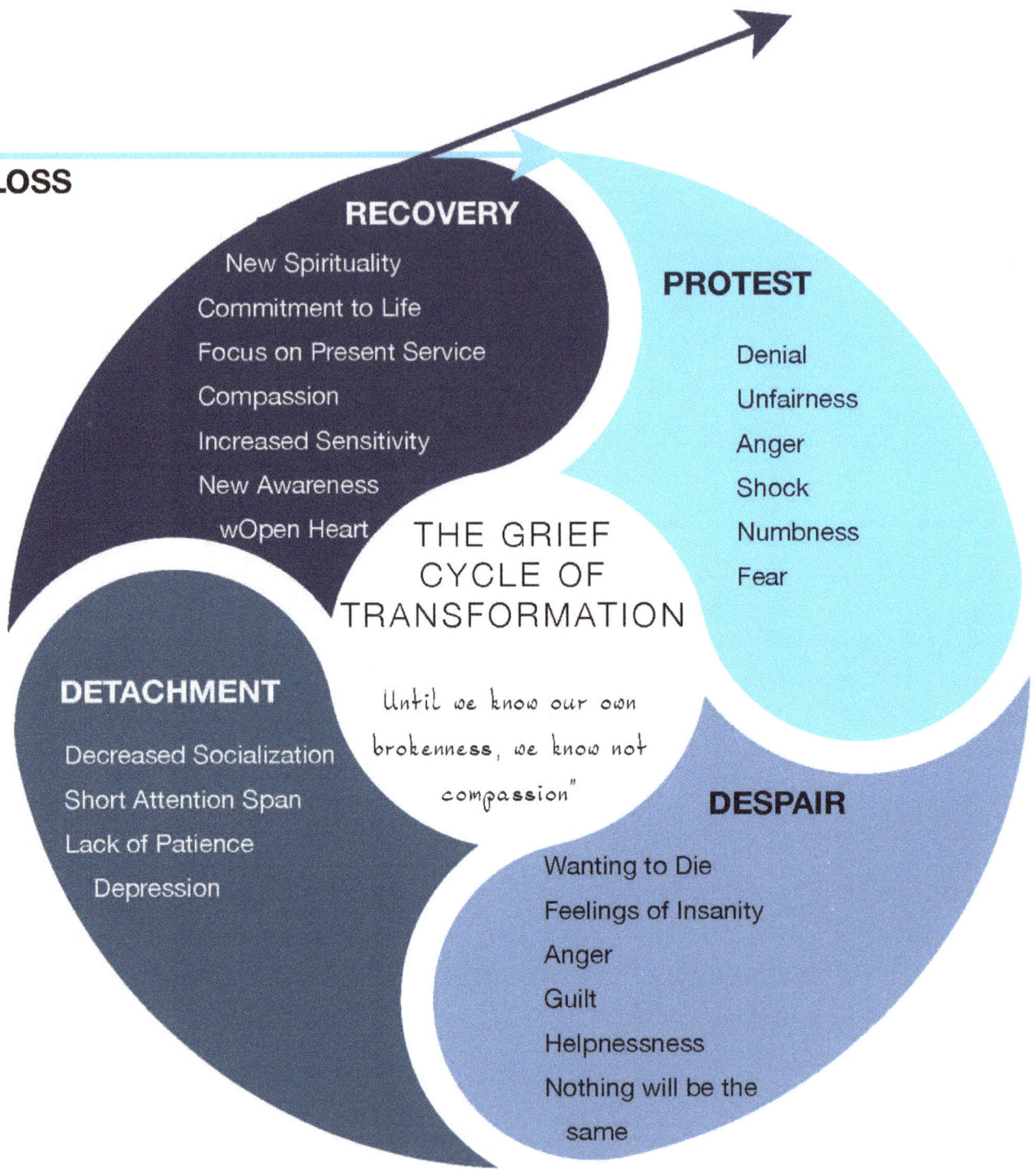

Adopted from the
Grief Education Institute

And you would accept the seasons of your heart, even as you have always accepted the seasons that pass over your fields. And you would watch with serenity through the winters of your grief.

~ Kahil Gibran, *The Profit*

Adjust to Your Environment

The third task of mourning is to convert the relationship with the deceased from one of presence to a relationship of memory. We must "adjust to an environment in which the deceased is missing," in the words of Davidson.

I recall the dreams I had of Dad. In those dreams, someone would bring him to our house for a visit, but we had to say goodbye. He always had to go back to wherever he had come from. The dream that was so very real for me was the one where Dad was standing behind the school yard fence. We could visit, but the fence separated us. As I grew older I realized the dream was my mind trying to understand my new relationship with Dad. It was one of memory.

Free - Intuitive Writing/The Unsent Letter

Some ways in which you can convert your relationship with your dear one is to use a writing technique that Rainer calls "Free-intuitive writing," where you empty your mind and hear with your inner ears. Be creative, treat the page as an open space, divide it, color it—be free. Rainer says, "The free-intuitive writing allows the hurt-child inner voice expression."

Write a letter to your loved one expressing what you couldn't do (regrets) because of his or her death, or all the things that you can do, and see yourself doing in the future. Express in the letter your strengths, your fears, and your desires. As a result of writing this unsent letter, you are more able to ease your mind and go on with your life, feeling that you have completed your side of the relationship. You can also use this journal technique to enter into the deceased person's point of view: "I'm sorry that you're hurting. I left because ..."

All of these suggestions aid in re-directing our emotional energies, bringing forth an adjustment of the psyche, and allowing the unconscious to assist in forming a new relationship with the deceased as one of memory.

Reinvest Emotional Energies

The fourth task of mourning is to develop a new self–identity based on a life without the deceased (Wolfelt), or to withdraw that emotional energy and reinvest it in other experiences and relationships (Davidson).

Life goes on and so did the lessons. I had lost who I thought I was. The form of what I had known as a relationship with my father was not there. I needed to reintegrate, and in that attempt I searched for meaning in life. There has been many a time when I have asked, "Why me?" and a small voice replied, "Why not you?" As I have matured, so has the grief. I believe in Steven Levine's concept that grief opens your heart. It certainly has opened mine. What I didn't realize at the time was that the gift Dad left me was not the new skirt and blouse in the birthday wrapping that day, but the rite of passage.

A Lesson in Every Goodbye

It is necessary to develop a new self-identity based on a life without the deceased. Utilize your experience as a stepping-stone that leads you forward. Remember that wave; it, like you, is a part of the ocean called Love-Intelligence. Your soul has been washed by the wave; move on and expand into each new day.

Tools, tools, tools, they are yours; give them a try—they assist you in providing a transcendent space in which to reflect and observe what has changed. "Reflection seems to occur when you stand back, even if only momentarily, and see the connections or significance that you had not noticed before," according to Rainer. "Sometimes reflections take the form of speaking directly to the self, or giving advice, encouragement, or bits of philosophic wisdom." Inner wisdom may make sounds like, "keep on keeping on," or "you can get through this." Many times the message that comes forth is a message that someone has already insisted on your getting, but when it comes from the self, it is yours to understand, not theirs.

Becoming aware of the roles that you played before the death, and the roles which you continued since the death, helps you to stand back and see the magnitude of change you have experienced. Asking questions like, "Who am I?" assists you in redirecting the emotional energy of pain into creative energy that provides a new relationship with self and others.

*WHO WAS I, AND
WHO AM I NOW!*

"Thought after thought, feeling after feeling, action after action. Now their target is gone. I keep on through habit fitting an arrow to the string; then I remember and have to lay the bow down."

~ C.S. Lewis, *A Grief Observed*

GIVE YOURSELF PERMISSION TO QUESTION YOUR BELIEFS

"Knock and it shall be opened." But does knocking mean hammering and kicking the door like a maniac?

~ C.S. Lewis, *A Grief Observed*

List Old Beliefs	List New Beliefs

WHAT BELIEFS HAVE GIVEN MY LIFE A SENSE OF MEANING?

Coping with the Holidays

(from the literature of MADD—Mothers Against Drunk Driving. Used with permission.)

You now face the holidays, and someone you love has died. At this time of year, intact families are everywhere—on television, in magazine ads, and on holiday cards, joyfully celebrating each other. You may feel swallowed in grief as you face a very empty chair at your table.

The following suggestions may help you cope.

- **Change traditions.** Have holiday meals and get-togethers at a different house or at a different time this year. The more you try to make it the same as it was before, the more obvious your loved one's absence will be.

- **Go away,** if you feel you will be devastated by staying home. But remember that Christmas is celebrated the world over, so you can't fully escape. You will probably do better by facing your pain and being near the people who love you.

- **Balance solitude with sociability.** Solitude can renew strength. Being with people you care about is equally important. Plan to attend some holiday parties, musicals, or plays. You may surprise yourself by enjoying it.

- **Relive the happy memories.** Pick three special memories of holidays past with your loved on. Think of them often—especially if grief spasms seem to pop up at inappropriate time.

- **Set aside "letting go" time.** Set aside on your calendar special times during the holiday season when you can be alone and grieve. When you know you will have these special times, you can more easily postpone your flow of grief in public.

- **Counter the conspiracy of silence.** Because family and friends love you, they will think they are doing you a favor by not mentioning your loved one (so you won't get upset). Break the ice by mentioning your loved one. Openly state it is important for you to talk about your loved one during the holiday season when he/she is so much on your mind.

- **Try not to "awful-ize."** It is tempting to conclude that life is "awful" during the holidays. Yes, you will have some difficult times—but you can also experience some joy. Experiencing joy in giving and receiving does not mean that you have forgotten your loved one or that you love him or her any less.

- **Don't forget the rest of your family.** Especially try to make it a good holiday for the children. Listen to them. Talk to them. Celebrate them. If decorating the tree or buying gifts is impossible, ask a friend to do it for you this year.

- **Take charge.** Plan ahead how you will handle issues, such as whether to hang your loved one's holiday stocking, whether or not to attend religious services, whom you will depend on for support.

You can't change the past. You can, however, take charge of the present. Total recovery may never come. But what you kindle from the ashes of your tragedy is largely up to you.

TEARS IN THE GRAVY

Mourning is giving myself permission to cry.

~ Dr. Patty Luckenbach

Relate the Experience of Loss to a Context of Meaning

The fifth task of mourning is "to relate the experience of loss to a context of meaning" (Wolfelt). This means "to formulate and reap a spiritual harvest from an understanding of immortality" (Davidson).

By expressing and writing down my feelings I have realized the process of grief is perfect, painful but perfect. I have been right on course as I have moved through the different stages. If we didn't hold on we wouldn't know to let go. We bridge the gap of polarity by dancing between the polarities of contradictory and confused experience to move toward the integration of our wholeness.

Understanding death and immortality has become my life's work. I make use of the memory of my father in my work with myself and others. His death was not in vain, for I have gained a new understanding. I have been able to lift the veil of separateness to sense the ever-expanding tapestry of life. Death truly is a spiritual journey, not just for the departed, but for each of us here on earth.

I have been given many gifts this lifetime: a harvest of blessings. One by one, they have built in me a deep conviction that goes beyond thought. My heart is open, no longer veiled in protection and defense, but open to the truth of the experience. When my words are silent, then the silence becomes words spoken.

8
RITUALS

All of life is a ritual.

~Jacquelyn O. Kennedy

Rites and rituals are ways to nurture our spirit. A rite or ritual fills the self, leaving no vacuums or empty places.

Thus, negativity has no place to enter or to exit.

- Sacred rituals make life more spiritual.
- Sacred rituals feed the self.
- When feeling pain or need, search out what is needed.
- Creation of a ritual provides for the healing.

A Ritual for Loss and Grief

A ritual for anything which interferes with head and heart:

- Choose a specific period of time
  - ❖ A week, 30 days, etc.

- Each day write what comes into your mind positive and negative
  - ❖ Roll the paper up and tie it with a ribbon
  - ❖ Place the scroll in a box

- Is there music or a fragrance which touches this issue?
  - ❖ Make these scents and sounds a part of your daily ritual

- Put your feelings into the writing
- Let the tears fall
- Release heavy sighs moans, shouts, screams, etc.
- When the time period is complete:
    - ❖ Bury the box, or
    - ❖ Burn the box and scatter the ashes

Do this ceremoniously!

- Candles are tools for ritual, rites, ceremony
    - ❖ They represent heat, light, and color.

- Oils with minerals and herbs, plus a scent, are tools. ~Notes from a workshop with Diana Velesquez, Cuerandera

RITUAL IS A
RITE OF PASSAGE

"*Either death is a state of nothingness and utter unconsciousness, or, as men say, there is a change and migration of the soul from this world to another. Now if death be of such a nature, I say that to die is to gain; for eternity is then only a single night.*"

~ Plato

WHO AM I NOW?

*What is my new self-identity based on a
life without him/her?*

What are ways I can stretch my wings?

"MOURNING NEVER ENDS, IT JUST ERUPTS LESS FREQUENTLY."

~Wolfelt

Dr. Ernest Holmes, Founder of the Church of Religious Science, had gone to San Francisco to see if he could get over his continued sense of loss after the passing of his wife, Hazel. And while sitting in meditation he heard from within himself these four statements:

"YOU WILL BE ALONE
UNTIL YOU ARE NO LONGER LONELY."

"YOU WILL LOOK AT DARKNESS
UNTIL IT BECOMES LIGHT."

"YOU WILL LISTEN TO THE SILENCE
UNTIL YOU HEAR IT SPEAK."

"YOU WILL DIE
UNTIL YOU RESURRECT YOURSELF."

~ From the unpublished works of Ernest Holmes

SUGGESTED READING

Adams, Kathleen, (1990). *Journal to the Self: 22 Paths to Personal Growth,* New York: Warner Books. Open the door to self-understanding by writing, reading, and creating a journal of your life.

Adler, Charles and Sheila, eds., (1976. *We Are But a Moment's Sunlight.* New York: Pocket Books, Inc. A collection of poetry and other selections from well known literature which give a universal perspective to the topics of death and bereavement.

Davidson, Glen, (1984). *Understanding Mourning.* Minneapolis: Augsburg Publishing House. A guide for those who grieve.

Grollman, Earl, ed., (1977). *Living When a Loved One Has Died.* Boston: Beacon Press. An inspirational book written in gentle poetic form; covers the stages of grief and the symptoms.

Herzog, Edgar, (1983). *Psyche and Death.* Dallas: Spring Publications, Inc. A book that explores death–demons in folklore, myths and modern dreams.

James, W. John; Cherry, Frank. (1989). *The Grief Recovery Handbook.* New York: Harper & Row, Publishers. A step-by-step program for moving beyond loss.

Levine, Stephen, (1987). *Healing Into Life and Death.* New York: Anchor Books, The book brings awareness of healing and embraced pain with mercy instead of fear.

Limbo, Rana; Wheeler, Sara: (1987). *When A Baby Dies.* LaCrosse Lutheran Hospital, Resolve Through Sharing, LaCrosse, WI. A handbook for healing and helping.

Moffort, Jane, (1980). *In the Midst of Winter.* New York: Random House. Describes the emotions of bereavement as experienced by mourners from all regions of the earth—from ancient times until the present.

Rainerm, Tristine, (1978). *The New Diary.* Los Angeles: J.P. Tarcher. How to use a journal for self-guidance and expanded creativity.

Richter, Elizabeth, (1986). *Losing Someone You Love: When a Brother or Sister Dies.* New York: Putnam's Sons.

In this book 15 young people who have lost a sibling talk openly about their feelings.

Tatebaum, Judy, (1980). *The Courage to Grieve.* New York: Harper. Combines summaries of research on grieving with personal experiences.

Toder, Francine, (1986). *When Your Child is Gone: Learning to Live Again.* Sacramento: Capital Publishing Co. This book is helpful for all parents who have lost a child through custody, kidnapping, death, adoption.

Westberg, Granger, (1978). *Good Grief.* Philadelphia: Fortress Press. Describes what happens to persons who lose someone or something important. Identifies 10 stages of grief.

Wolfelt, Alan, (1983). *Helping Children Cope with Grief.* Munci: Accelerated Development, Inc. Written for parents, teachers and counselors who have both a desire and a commitment to help children when they experience death.

The Eagle represents a state of grace achieved through hard work. Grief is hard work and Stephen Levine, stated, "Grief is like holding to a rope as it is pulled through your hand." The Eagle represents an understanding, and a completion of the test of initiation which results in the taking of one's personal power. Grief is emotional pain from having experienced a change and loss and from this experience can be the greatest of all initiations. It is only through the trial of experiencing the lows in life as well as the highs, and through the trials of trusting one's connection to life, that the right to use the essence of the Eagle's qualities is earned. Take heart and gather your courage.

The raptors such as the hawk can imbue you with the power to overcome a stressful, difficult situation. It can give to us the courage to enter the darkness of the void, and to allow our personal integrity to guide us and sustain us and to allow the feeling of aloneness to vanish at the perfect moment. Allow courage to circle your head and heart.

NOTES

www.ingramcontent.com/pod-product-compliance
Lightning Source LLC
Chambersburg PA
CBHW042339030426
42335CB00030B/3409